The PiNDER POET

MARY LOUiSE VAUGhN ShiRLEY hOPSON

COME TASTE
The SUGARCANE —

A ViEW

FROM The STAiRCASE

WiTh DiALOGUE

Palindrome Publishing of Iowa

1ˢᵗ edition, 1ˢᵗ printing

© 2004 by ML Hopson
with permission to Palindrome Publishing of Iowa to publish
& Sheridan Books to print

ISBN: 0-9720717-1-7
Library of Congress Catalog Number:
2004103453

Palindrome Publishing of Iowa / West Des Moines, Iowa

Cover and layout design by Karisa Runkel

Photography by Timeless Images Photography, Donna Rayne

Manufactured by Sheridan Books, Inc.

ACKNOWLEDGEMENTS

I am grateful to my parents, Robert and Sadie Cornelius Shirley Vaughn, for teaching me to live both in my space and out of it, to adapt to changes in one's life and to my childhood friend, Eloise Anderson Russell, USAF, (now deceased) who mentored me, protected me from bullies while growing up in Gowdy, Mississippi, and recommended me for every job that she had, leading me to Iowa. Also, I want to thank my many friends and professional colleagues who have embraced me and supported my writings: Linda and Jerry Skeers, Tammy Hurley, Reverend Jimmie Horton (a fellow Gowdian), John Gaps III, Barry Benson, Phil Hey, Pat Underwood, Karen Jobst, and Arthur Neis as well as the following poetry groups: Omega Poetry Group; Iowa PEN Women; the Great Society of River Poets of Burlington, Iowa; and the Plymouth Church Poetry Project of Des Moines.

"LANGUAGE IS

POWERFUL AND

COMPELLING

WHEN IT EVOKES

A RESPONSE."

—M.L. HOPSON,
The PINDER POET

Notes on Translations and Title

*Come Taste The Sugarcane—A View From the
Staircase With Dialogue* has been like a
reoccurring mantra since childhood as I still hear
ancient voices of my ancestors who came under
the whip-aboard ships, boats to settle in many
lands of the world as they carried in their pouches
rootstock to plant, to gather, to press into
sweetness. The stalk, their hope; their dialog to
express in tongues of their origins: Swahili,
Afrikaans, Cajun French (Brazilian), and
Portuguese. Their desire as commodities brokers
was to share sweetness in places where the
rootstock grew: A distiller to blend with others to
taste and engage in dialogue wherever the
boundary or language spoken – Hindi, Russian,
Hawaiian, Thai, Chinese, or Welsh.

The phrase "come taste the sugarcane" is a
blender, a translation in commonality of
rootstocks to alter conflict, and to chew and taste
with ease among cultures of every rank, root or
hue with dialogue to view.

Mary Louise Vaughn Shirley Hopson
The Pinder Poet

Come

Njo kuhonja Sukari ya miwa

Taste

Kom proe die suikerriet

The

Venez gouter la canne á sucre

Sugarcane

Venha experimentar a cana deçúcar

Come Taste the Sugarcane

FOREWORD

M.L. Hopson's life as a poet has traversed several hemispheres without ever leaving mainland America: the hemispheres of North and South, white and color, woman and man, adult and child. Professor C. Leigh McInnis, Professor of English at Jackson State University, writes of Hopson, "Being an African-American, just in existence, is a unique existence from any other experience on the planet. This is not to say that we do not have universal or common human experiences. But this is to acknowledge and understand that to be people who were imported into the country to be slaves and to be freed with the country having no plan or concept as to what to do with us after slavery has created a complex existence for us, never fully affirmed as citizens in a country that we had an equal part in developing. It means loving a country that does not love you. Yet, it also means turning the most nasty, decayed, spoiled, and soured lemons into the sweetest lemonade, rivaled only by the wine produced at the wedding by Jesus. Our existence on this land is likened to a beautiful flower bursting through concrete. Just as Nature must continue to survive and evolve, so have we proven to be just as steadfast and diligent. This is the central issue in M.L. Hopson's work."

Hopson's latest book of poetry, *Come Taste the Sugarcane—A View from the Staircase With Dialogue* continues where her critically acclaimed, seminal book, The Pinder Poet: Cherishing This Heritage began with insightful, poignant lyricism and commentary about the complexity of being an individual, a race, a people in the United States of America. Hopson is a master of cultural storytelling and one of the finest performance poets our nation has to offer.

Content

CONTENT

COME TASTE THE SUGARCANE

When the wrath of wars' wail
causes rage, drips tears, fears,
puts a levy upon men,
women, children who fall under
wrack and wreck to endure--
roots loss to crush, squander, consume.

Stage a misery-quenched role,
an explosion in horror, sorrow,
terror, trauma, imprisonment, drama.

Where a war zone becomes
our taste, our chew, our fate
to negate, go after and allow heaviness
to soften, withdraw. Blench out
grief, breakaway our bereavement.

Sight treasure chests for warfare
in advance, a hoist upon shoulders
by some who create such weight.

Strike, follow trails that lead
into patches: propagate, proliferate
stalks to grow sweetness.
Shape and support sugar mills
that process sugariness as a treaty for peace.

Come with me into the field
taste what's plowed with your foot
amongst common people, lay people,
redesign spaces, riches, niches,
and commit to memory how to
cultivate grazing lands sown with sugariness.

Transport stalks of sweetness, and
restructure harsh environments into landscapes
of Green Nirvana.

hiE RARChy

Lingam tree
bones hide
inside a seed

Moon in Capricorn
angel chorus
gifts of Yoni

Stars blink magic
orb stilled
cries afar

Awaken soothsayers
words chant--
bleat of the lamb

Lilies trumpet
earth shakes
rivers pour out

On the bough
avifauna perch
holy chirps hail

Songs of Babylon
ascending mountains
babble utter miracles

HOODWINKING

An ol' possum
On a spit you say?

Before I can turn this trick
Shouldn't the idea be
Thought out glanced o'er a bit?

Not being one
To straddle a limb

While Blue Tick Hounds
Make moves as you take aim

Can't you jes" ignore?:
Stay those barkers at bay?
I ain't use to dis' playing dead
Nor as vittles upon a table spread

Now this can't be yo' doin'
A notion to imbibe
I ain't ready to be surrounded
By yams, onions, greens, turnips, garlic

Let alone these yellow dogs
And Blue Tick Hounds

Tell me

How did this Southern cuisine
Become such a epicureanosity
An imitate for a Northern fling?

Why this southern imbibination
To court a Northern invitation?

Now look what you'd done
Teehee! Hee! Teehee! Hee!
I say you've got me tree'd
Yo' done got me tree'd

Ah woof! Woof! Ah! Woof Woof!
I've been treed
And it sho' ain't what I need

A GLASS OF LADY CHABLIS IS BEING SERVED AT MIDNIGHT IN THE GARDEN

He had been her paramour.
A liaison naught to resist,
as dyads they lingered to meet
amidst labyrinths of intrigue.

Now he stumbles
upon an exposure,
a pose in reverse.

As an aftermath of cold creeps, seeps,
a secrecy of darkness uncovers circumstances
not rehearsed as he succumbs to distress
upon seeing her out-stretched
inside a glass hearse.

There she lies in her tomb,
as a moondog guards from afar
sending glimmers of moonlit nips
to whomever dare come to take a sip.

Now John's sorceress reposes
inside a silk-lined crepe de chine chest
where he soon joins her,
in composure.

He reclines in silk habiliments
after sniffing thallium flowers lying beside her
for hours and hours.

THE NAUGHTY IDIOT-LECTIC

He eats peas on a knife
While dining with his wife
A fluff of a hindered mouthpiece

He is a bit of a swine
With a runt of a mind
Who grunt and hurl insults

While his children shudder
As they placate and utter
Response to his being

He throws rations upon their plates
Misused gestures to intimidate
As he wallow in his slop

His irrational conduct with threats
When expectations not met
Placing intellect aside he shifts

His tongue to deride
His reason aside
And he "hiss"

Soon encountering demise
His wife, an uncommon surprise
Whom he called like a dog in heat

Or a pudendum some might say
But that not his way
with so limited words

Provocation induces a plot
To dis-com-bob-u-late this dolt
She reaches extreme

At hand, she fetches a box filled
With feline slime pitched as he sprawled
SPLASH! Watch as he sputters

Slouched, spattered into limbobosity
Restrainer words lisped from civility
Words drawn to dismiss

UNFOLDING

A Prophet thunder, voice strokes, reverberates-
Binds minds into desperation, captive, they linger to
Commune; with limbs crossed, petitioning for salvation,
Depths of living, unmask loss-bearing sensations.
Ether emits, sends libations'
Flames to ignite some ape-men, as followers

Howl-O-Lu-Ya!

Gather like lambs, enter every cultural center;
Havens bloom like mustard seeds
Into patches thatched with needles borne from
Judgmental deeds, like trees that hold moisture:
Kaleidoscopic outpourings of sweat, our tears, holystones
Laden with drips, drips flowing like
Mantles of mist or a mirage seen on ocean dunes-
Nothing nothing but refusal to consume.

Howl-O-Lu-Ya!

O how winds howl like roving wolves
Passing through narrow paths in droves
Quick as leaves from quaking trees, intermingle --
Resting, nesting onto ground fallow
Still beneath hard crust, seams crack, swallow, and grow
To tile, then tilled to kill as never before.

Howl-O-Lu-Ya!

Underneath where Helios penetrates,
Violence erodes, loam raises quakes
While robots equate to monitor fate,
X-ray secrets open to annihilate.
Yaws becomes semen seed, sown AIDS in taste--
Zees soon negate to contaminate, recycle waste

THE FRETWORK HAND
OF THE CLOCK
MOVES PAST THE HOUR

As I prepare to ask?

"O father, why do you speak
So often of someone, of those
    I do not know?"

But, to daring reproach,
From one who begot
    this olive branch--

To utter, 'Should I?' and, 'Should I?'

When at last I spoke
The voice timid
Shifted from low to high,
Then back again to reply.

The clock ticks,

"Mending thoughts,
I now know of whom he knew."

My eyes move in transit
To gaze at the matriarch,
To see laced upon her frame
All that could be, always to sustain-
-

A bee, prophetess, wife, woman

Buried under the "Oak of weeping."

Miss Annie Mae's Chapeau

Every summer Sunday afternoon
Past azaleas, peonies, crepe myrtles
She would stroll with her beau
Who held onto her hand
As if it were Waterford or Lalique.

She wore her topper
Like a fancy showstopper,
Tilted and perched
With fabric of silk, raffia, tulle
That never flipped or flopped
Should the wind play
In a whimsical way.

She was a head turner who wore
A dress to match with organza
Lace and all that "Jazz"
Creating a razzamatazz along the way
As flora took a bow as they flung
Their fragrance to acknowledge
That they were there

Braiding honeysuckle vines into a twine
We children shadow play, skip one jump, and two jump
Over petals, moss, four-leaf clover, scented poesies

Miss Annie Mae and Mister Shelley
Making cardinals, warblers sing
Him with his top hat and her
With her flip of a bonnet

DRINKING FROM THE MISSISSIPPI: MUD OF MY BONES AND GRIT

With potency my father pours
While mother fills up to fortify
This elixir of power that flows

I a branch float up, wade around
In this torrent of determinism

I am a forager, tadpole, crawl fish
A slough of shells, a floating buttress against swells
That rises to emerge like granite.
Some offspring defy being awash
Upon flotsam streams, search for dreams
Drift into imagined scenes, swim forward
Onto places seen, nor seen.
Ancestors a distant before
Whose ticket on foodstuff and drink
Rationed gave flavor to woe
Gathered together
Stranded beyond a jetsam shore.

Free, I am summer's dry wrap
Whose skin scorches, bones rip
Between quandaries, quagmires move
To push pebbles against think tanks,
But not to swallow or wallow among
Those who bathe in downpours, only
To gulp assumptions, presumptions,
On thoughts that grab soon stab.

Look at me in full view.
My frame imposes strength of will
Sculpted against waves, tides that flow
Wanderlust of trust to journey
Over sand, gravel, rift, silt

"I've seen Rivers."

I am this scavenger
River artillery, my watercourse
Rafting, hunting through waterways,
Far away, still.

HOW SHOULD i PEEL THIS ONION

Whose center
Whiff's desire
As I touch and twirl

My savor of tang so acute
That I can detect an odor
Of mephitis in clean upscale
Restaurants in Omaha
Or the Taj Mahal

Is this the hour to slash

This layer of hunger to squash
A mess of onion with patchouli emitting
A need felt under the afterglow
Of a passionate orgiastic moon,

To unpeel like scabs on a pimple
A blood blister to chop
Singe into a last chance
As a weight on the mind
Scrapes, then seeps, making
Thoughts edgy as a pit bull's snarl

While I chop, slice
Carve away aroma sucked into nostrils
Inhale exhale stench of gamy savor

APOLOGIZE FOR SUBJUGATION? ITS THIS DISFRANCHISEMENT THAT TRICKLES

"When we unbind ourselves
From slavery within."
                    Nicholas Berdyaev

O hear preceptors vocalize
Their dialogue revokes corroboration
As some endorse to undermine
Most places recounted in time.

"By the book" is taught—
How hatred beat drums—
Yet to speak of destiny, confounds
Where paths renders a slow down
Over novel spooling approaching equality
When tracks froth in antiquity
Still wakes trail. Open, coast
As some travel to boast,
While others speak to negate
One's contest, an equal to assimilate.

Though faces darkened, a course-book
Whose text is whitened in chronicles?
Of dim messages, fixed in recall…

Soon cast as dawdling, if one
Should contemplate that cut-off stumps
Shall be their seats, or avowed ownership

Share a compliance to defeat,

JULIA'S CHAPEAU UPON THEIR TOPS THEY WORE

Mister John, Aldolfo, Dior, Hattie Carnegie—
Those artisans sought through corroboration
While poodle skirts were showoffs
Worn posh, sketched to detail rhinestone
Leashes simulating a dogtrot.

Along came a trendsetter, a jewel
Crowned most renown, her taste in haute couture,
Propensity, an interest to serve elites with style
Creations to flatter and accessorize

Whether at an opera or soiree—
A notion that pleased they wore at ease.
Such designs tended refined that suited

Swell, like modes of Mesdames Miller, Lehman, Finkbine
Ladies evaluated as affluent, influential
Like mink, most essential, yet

Inclinations toward vanity were not
Avant garde, Art Deco or Art Nouveau
As consuming interventions—

An art, though smart to boot

Liberation, an exposure, as noir was vogue,
Out-Of-season after fives

Became out-moded frocks,
To Julia's cottage, who's-who flocked,
Where off came elevated heels

Fore-going style for comfort
While high fashions were purchased
To mold shapes, panoply to blend,

Flourishing looks that dazzled with flair.
She spoke with an edge cemented concise,
Savvy her obsession toward this

Determined breed whom she draped
Into knockouts where some were
Headliners on boardwalks.

Knowing what was what, she showed
Them how to strut their stuff

As they strolled Avenues along the Seine
Savored caviar in Milan, and purchased
Pricey paintings in Spain

While turning on allure for their spouses.
Carry-on liquidated assets on hand,
Currency tucked inside their purses
Passports around the universe to cruise

Along coral reefs, into some places to herald bands,
High-borns known and unknown,
From Fort Dodge, Perry, Pisgah, Podunk, Redfield

She clothed in brocades, chiffons,
Silk up to the ilk, pisante, shantung's
Oleg Cassini, Geoffrey Beene to Molly Parnis,

Originals scoring an exclusive appearance—
H.H. Sondheim, Pierre Balmain, Coco Channel.
Yet not to forget Jackie O., princess of Camelot

Who was a focus of class distinction
In chemises, faille, lamé, pearls.
O Julia was bold

Top dogging likes, dislikes
Into a reason to emancipate
Their brains out of clinches:

Don't save it for the second wife,

I'm third was heard—

A legend if it were told.
She brought women to their senses
Where perseverance was lame
When it came to wear black

Or dress out in flame
Steeped in Iowa Gold.
Their legacy through dress was select

An era presented to raise skirts
Above or below knees.
Fashions were the glitter—

Portrait for a New Yorker or Sioux Citier.
O Julia was a mentor, like Warhol to looks
She was not a clotheshorse

Or a wall to hang a rack.
This lady oozed tact to attract
Championing many who opted
To don pants or wear sheaths that hung loose,

Never a glove misplaced
Or a skirt to be ruin by length—

Not even a fiasco as an event on the hill
When two matrons of class
Their entrance to cause a stir

From the stairs descending wearing
Look-alike Matisse prints, but not in pink
Making the hostess with the mostest shrink.

But Julia's favor,
Her reputation for one of a kind,
Was style-power evident, succinct—

Would never have caused such a waggish
incident.
Cloche, toques, Scaperreli
Dressings from Fifth Avenue, Seventh Avenue

Were fashion pleasers, style teasers
To score like music or a dance
Wherein the Heartlands elegance:

An intent to top the haute monde into
Stunning cultural attire at a glance.

WHAT MEANING DOES THIS PRESAGE?

I say.
Who's that ah' pecking on this wall,
Rap'tap'tatting yo' mournful wakeup
call?

Fo' O Helios is on the rise,
You come 'round tapping this site;
Weren't yo' wings ever clipped,
You 'ole' top' of scarlet, in a glide?

Don't go around so early
Feeding yo' craw,

Rap! Rapping yo' tap
Perhaps you can't help yoself'.

Cogitating my demise 'uh! uh!
In the morn before day arise,
You come glidin' to scrounge
Through this thicket?

What
 A postulating assumption.

Stay closer, let me spit
A royal purple plant in your eye,
Want you to know
I ain't ripen enough to die.

Though a shriveling vine,
I don't intend to change 'til' due time,

Shoo! Shoo! You fake magpie, you!

Y'ALL COME CYBERING WITH ME

I's a browser as I graze through cyberspace,
Brushability is my game when I search throughout
For the whereabouts of brunizem

O away with dials yo' hold gainst' ears
Can grow old on hold as yo' utter
Words ya' hear:
Sneers, clicks, no tones, screeches,

Which causes jolts of brusquerie if you dare
Intrude, such arrogance this bucko biz,' risk being
Cloned a brute to spin as a buffoon
Who suffers buck fever, or a bucksaw gnawing
On a bassoon.

But on the Net one can join a salsa set
Cyber to discuss da'Met
Meet Bill's as you scan through mates,
Chat through spats
Can ignore a dull bloke faceless
Who tell jokes
As going sleeveless in Siberia
Chillin' out to smoke.

OLE' grannies scan through Seniornet
To scout aah' cruise
Where either can do a buck-and-wing
Or join a karaoke partee' to sing,
"Nothing like an oldster"
Grown bolder da' tune
"I placed a bet on the Internet,"
Scroll a mouse, boot a lout
Who ignores a TOS

Surf murf, drink Smirnoff,
Cappuccino, tea or coke
Send e-mail, order a snail, smell an rat
Who clicks to chat
Gnaw and chew over the news,

Placate a simpering fool
Loop da' Web over Timbuktu and Tibet
Glance at Japan,
Taipan and Zululand
Scroll on da' way to Pakistan,
Rhoumidan,
Then surf to Toga land.

Perch on a chair anywhere
Be an elephant-tusk
Or donkeys-rear
Who can fart and not
Smell up the hemisphere,
While digits do da' trot
Whar' eyes reveal da' spots dat' sizzle
Drizzle or fizzle.

Ya'll can be aah' democratic nerd
A nude who sits before a screen
With a modem dat' broadcast
Wheezes, groans, with erratic stops,
Locks and pops.
If yo' choose, can be ah' looker
Who view a hooker
To gawk,
Salivate til' jaws lock.
Or shop for BVD's, motor ease
Until yo' drop

I's aah' yowl yowl browser,
A download whizzer
On how to build a Kayak,
Control a Bat;
Seeking the denizen of the deep
From the woo, woo world,
Accessing mo' mo' bytes
Than you can snake a pipe.
Lol Lol! Yall.

NEW AGE WOMAN
UNOER AN OLO
CORE CURRICULUM, STILL

A gala of impulses, an in-trend
Her idiosyncrasy, powerfulness to end
A swoon d' affair whose intent
To land as a knockout
On Mister Blackwell's list

Gambits with flair to wear
Breast shot corsage like Tyra
That would orchestrate either rage
Over ethos that promote lust
On one's taste bought or sold
Bold in slinks, sequins, diamonds, furs
That spark more winks than blink
On a Las Vegas marquee.

Earned affluence assures expanse spinning
To slot-in on casino spending
Binges to engage in flings
Eclipsing dassiness sassiness of La Liz,
Oh Oh Oh! J. Rivers, Cher, J Lo, Divine Midler
Coloratura migrants of fall winter
Summer spring.

Showtime fashions do-cinch
Into Dior, Versace, Yves St. Laurent,
Vintage sintinge of Betsey Johnson to view
More rags on racks than you can buy
From Junior Leaguers carry-on-bags
Their bargain door as some
Do-styles to beguile lesser known
Advocates who ruffle pages
Of Elle, Vanity Fair, O, Cosmopolitan
Town & Country, Women's Wear.

Faction of the pack
As some traveling fair from Wal-Mart's
T J Maxx, Sax & Sak.

The haute couture for the haute monde
Who don T-Eyes then strut their stuff
On Avenues of LA, Belize, Paris, Reno, Cancun
With such razzes to dazzle
On walkways of the Mall
Showtime gallivants wiggle jiggle waggle
In the spotlight wearing wash-n-wear
Unnecessary to dress like wimps
Seen as trophy trinkets
To dispel or to invite exaggerated glimpse
Wearing hoity toity naughty rags
Raveling in look-a-like flags—
Create fashion news for tongues
That wag wage wig and wag

OBSERVATiONS VARiATiONS iN VERSE

NATIONAL APOLOGY
We ask to bind a wound
but you wrap us in gauze
laced with microorganisms cloaked
in noxiousness, an act causing pain

ENEMY
You dart arrows
tips poisoned with juice siphoned
from the dogbane tree
but we hold the armor
to deflect this missile of hate

LOVERS
A confession poured
like acid flowing through
a sieve, did nothing
but strain my ardor

ON LIARS
Through the mouths of prevaricators
flow the sludge of Beelzebub

ON POLITICS
While the lecturer serializes
and minds race through
tracks of rhetorical slubber
politics rush beyond
our organ of hearing

PROMISCUITY
Women hair rippled with curls
staring at the world
spread legs to divulge
more than is necessary

PLUNDERER
More than an apology
is necessary when you create
and promote disorder

DEATH WEARS A MASK

Some places circumstance becomes a curdle
To nibble as mildew reproduces shapes
Where map outs show humanity
In the company of starvation
To witness flesh in doorways at rest.

Soon doors and entrances close
as all eyes shift then shun
those who lie upon beds
wrapped in stain bandages of need.

Beggars rise; pull tons of grub from rubbish
as hunger hums a groan.
Inside their bellies, a grumbling tempo of pride
whither, as poverty elicits. "Why?"

Time spent to make a dollar holler
a buck a quarter, buys nothing.

Lights invades, then dims within gaps
To follow noon into dimness,
where brothers gather outside housings
As wealth flashes by
Zoom! Soon you hear rants, organizing
among bloodsuckers, a ruckus.

Sisters suffer moving in holding areas,
bellow like herds of buffalo
while their children, thin as plucked
chickens, squawk about neglect.

The air reeks with the odor
Of corpses lying about a city of predators
While bank fronts, Shadow Governments. Operates
in long lines flourished through blame
as death wears a mask.

Ode to Johnnie Ruth

O Johnnie Ruth, child of dread,
Where did you throw your baby doll?

"In a ditch behind the shack,
In a ditch behind the shack"

But why, O Sweet Johnnie Ruth,
Child of distress? Why?

What charmer did you obey,
Who made you throw your
Newborn doll away…

In a ditch behind the shack?
In a ditch behind the shack?

"Alone I did bear
A being I could not fondle"

Alone, O Sweet Johnnie Ruth, alone.
Why do you tremble so?

"A seed of dishonor, my act with him
Who with play led me astray, why

I threw it away…threw it away!
Threw my baby doll away!

In a ditch behind the shack…
In a ditch behind the shack."

IN MOTHER'S BED
A BOUQUET OF THORNS

A babe is born, whose flesh rankles with scorn
Where purity of bloodline flows, spoils
In mother's bed a bouquet of thorns

A rape seed through gender a pit is sown
Now alone she endures, back stretch in toil
A babe is born, whose flesh rankles with scorn

Poverty confines, clones, a briar grown
To bear over patches a ward from sperm oil
In mother's bed a bouquet of thorns

Soon suffering arise render jolts, reborn
Into a state to abandon, neglect, recoil
A babe is born, whose flesh rankles with scorn

A child alone whose father unknown
As they await the signature, a bitter foil
A babe is born, whose flesh rankles with scorn

Another delivery whose base is born
A beginning to lie down in a vat that boils

A babe is born, whose flesh rankles with scorn
In mother's bed a bouquet of thorns

An Equidistant-Aged Lady On The Verge Of Not Becoming A Curmudgeon -ess

I have sucked lemons over time
And drank chalices of consecrated wine
A lifestyle forced to experience decline
Set in motion by those with an arrogant eye
Whose views to shape stifle a cry

Although my perception of those who offend
Has not bent my shoulders or maxed-out my senses
As the rift continues to drift and flow
From crevices far above and below
My spine built like a flying buttress
On the verge, not becoming a curmudgeon-ess

Though I still climb stairs steep
My foot steps a slow determined creep
As floors become a wide open drop
I step, shift forward to avoid a spot
Where so many have gone before
To squeeze through ceremonies of a padlock door
Always to "play a waiting game" but no more
Roots rooted in slavery suffrage denial and pain

I cry! I cry! Let's all join and mentor to gain
Gray skulls of every hue tone place or shape
Let the anthem of insistence open our gate
To us who will not accept less
 of becoming an equidistant comurdgeon-ess

BURY ME NOT iN This LONE CAMPGROUND

Will they dump my remains with no name,
Scattered upon waste deposit grounds,
Where wild weeds and wreckage gains;

A tomb nonetheless rife with shame,
A tangle wood that's choked and bound?
Will they dump my remains with no name.

No taps, nor hymns, neither carriage train --
Only whirl of flies a buzzing sound,
where wild weeds and wreckage gains.

When you were twenty-two a buck of a frame,
in shanties, melted medicine men peddled their rounds.
Will they dump my remains with no name?

Twenty-five cents a week for burial they sang,
While Ma & Pa sat in their rockers, their thoughts a frown,
Where wild weeds and wreckage gains.

Shall this be our resting place, their refrain,
as they stood up and cried "Why?" This devil's pound
...
Will they dump my remains with no name
Where wild weeds and wreckage gains?

OVARiMONY:
"MEN hAVE ThEiR TESTiMONY
WOMEN ThEiR OVARiMONY..."

My blood flows
every twenty-eight days.
Without being stabbed
I suffer
pangs of your urge
like a knife
thrust
between thighs
resurrected
in displeasure.
Your sweat
does not make
my butterfly flutter
as you rise
bang poke breathe
convulsive
explosions,
moan:
"Oh God! O God!
I'm coming I'm coming
as I moan
"O God! Let me die."
Your ecstasy
becomes my pain
with strokes of lust
miasma misery
abandonment.
Afterwards I lie
upon my bed of tears.
An outward act
becomes an inward act
of staged drama
to let loose/ link up
with a human race of fear
of war, AIDS, neglect
genocide-
a lone pacifier of death
to suck

DIALOGUE

Shall breeding options to plot
Block the stage for alterations
In how we choose our
Meat and bones in butcher shops

To clone when men confront
Women with their penile humor
That engulfs as if every breast,
Hip, clitorisorial mount is their
Imperialist throne to own?

OUR ANCESTORS
SLAVE IMMIGRANTS
CALL US ON THIS JOURNEY
A WALK INTO THE MILLENNIUM

To see specks, scowls trace
Lines raked across brows,
Twisted upon countenances to convey
Moments revealed, take a surrey ride
Toward destiny to forfeit what
Passed before, only to hear
Cogwheels make clack! Clacking sounds,
Scrolling beats of a runaway blood pump.

Seat of passion resounds, offer reparation,
Cast light below, draw breaths of lore
That across some seacoast blew, rootstock
From where began this roundabout
Through olive branches planted
Sown between dimness some triumphs

Words spoken as truth
Marks affixed in legend told
A textile of the soul.

From early bondage, stick figures
Landed by trade, architects, moved
Settled to drop anchor under whips,
Mastered sites with imprint of the
Dark Continent etched across their brow.

Caught up in the view
See faces carved in friendship
As they journeyed into virgin
Landscape, shoulders bent, soil toiled,
Bricks shaped that tiled roads,
Steel fondled then molded into rods
To prop up domiciles.

Inherited hands imagined, stroking life
Offering a pennon of trust
Pulling blocks for so many
When pats or shakes tampered
Minds with offers, discarded
Remnants, torn fragments scattered,
Hampered by drags of constraints

Beyond groves an excursion, past trails
Moored havens, crimped areas to range
Where century old buildings stand, beckons, still
Sit stretched into the millennium
Along river bends, their place
Amidst authorized terms of traverse.
Aftertime now walks along tracks.
Step deep into anchored footprints
Wear the imprint, string hope, and carry deed
Bow before forefathers, foremothers
Come inside portals to trek
Restored around habitats
Keeping villages intact.

it speaks and
it is more than a picture i see

I close my eyes
Take a digit and place
it upon the screen

I feel a throb
As the mind scan
began to trace imagined tracks seen

The finger began to climb
Like a foot digging into crevices
An arm stretch like a rope
to grab striving for the top

Still descending I watch for narrow ridges,
ears tuned to speculate the baa! baaaaaa!
of the mountain goat as it leaps from crag to crag

Still upwards to feel truth
that raised hills are still there,
and that yips of coyotes still echo
Picture mule deer baying in the distance

Something jars me
It is my heart beating
like a runaway blood pump

I open my eyes to see
My hands out-stretched
across the computer screen
as if to hide from realization

A refrigerator door opens sending cool air
I see snow capture the color of bile
Once a mountain now looks like
Man made humps hollowed abandoned mines
The topography in its coldness void of life
The light I see in the distance is nothingness invading
The orb and old Helios has disappeared
through the haze pine trees stumps
appear as burnt shrubs disintegrating
And windmills their whirls silent
as extinct as birds-of prey

DiMiNiSheD PASTURES

We come to graze upon grasses
Sown by apostles with their cultivated
Gestures, dispiriting notions planted in bare soil.
Then tiled under eroded indulgences--
Quicksand like a silent sermon,
Not easy to recoil
Zephyr, whose rumble mimic a deity of change
Gathers rootlets, blows embryonic grains
Of unity to scatter among cities.
Fountainheads, open reservoirs, flow
Into fields where tunnels becloud, yield to let loose
In their fury, transformation:
To unleash hostages
Tacked onto prairies of urbanization,
Heap filtered taste of realization...
After the deluge

GIRCH AND POWER STRING
CHEIR ELECTRICAL WORLD

Metal art form along highway 218
Victorian shaped transformers like puppet pulls
Stretching pulling lines and doing time

Heedless under man's prerogative
They look to the heavens
And glitter like stars
As though their place decoded
Among the ancient

This family unit as cloned sisters
A medium of materialization
Copper, clamps, rivets, voltages
Charge through currents upon
Shoulders girded in steel
To hold liquid fire and air
Aluminum Georgettes, nippleless bosoms
Solomon's seal lace their frames

No breasts, gears to clutch at whim
Nor expressions to tantalize

Armed with Old Testament bearing energy
Waists cinched in metered girdles
Skirts tic-tac toe'd where you can
Gaze upon countryside, maize, legumes, clover
Cylinders of fodder as livestock graze
On either side bulls bay, horses neigh

WHEN THEY SEE
A CAMERA
THEY SMILE

Children among the masses
Wear a world of suffering as a
Mirror image in their eyes
As they rummage around seeking
For loveliness

Where cheeks, limbs that limp
Are pockmarks for poverty
Abuse, neglect, rape of war,
Hunger and traumas not to forget

Through the lenses a cameo
For the world to see to exploit
As they grin to hide their misery

SOME LEARN EARLY
(how To Milk A Cow)

By jes' a pull on der' teats
ta' squeeze 'til dry
as ef' an endless supply
now dat' pail don' run ova'
no mo' ta' give no
smack o' dos' lips
all yo' wan',

Dis' time da intimidato'
has close' da' dairy.
Dose' tits once swell wid'
milk ta' cash in on
when yo' pucker yo' lips
In na' aah' satisfyin' grip.

No mo' milk fest
Wealth fes',
top-o'-cream
fes' to suck.

I's sorry, but you
mus' be told
No mo' "I got milk"
in dis' udder's bag
for yo' sucker fes'
from da'
gov's nes'.

TRIFLE FLAPPING
NETWORKING

How you doing

See those bagatelles
with their intensified
wavers on demand
where swarms of
entitlements surfaces
commands

All that narrative
Hyperbole plunges into
macrocosmic held forums

Where some inside
outside rappers drum
to smoke-out bees

Senses waxes like
honeycombs, but lack
hives to store

Soon turn into
drips of blurbs
that seep puffs
buoyed past time,

Reason stalls into
The millennium to accompany
shallow dawdlers who
opt to drown
in grips of idolatry.

You know what I'm saying?

I'M GONNA TAKE YOU
WHERE YOU'VE NEVER BEEN BEFORE,
ENJOY. CAN YOU FEEL IT?

An appliqué of impulses ignites
When a milkweed puff upon brushwood
Inside an outhouse is tossed
The onset of a flare sets off
To put to test an article to sprinkle
A target not to miss

Profuse this use since Eve
In all places known
Where the pisser has trickle
To stir in the wind
To rise like fury
At the moment of yen
To dribble upon oats spun
As it zing zag, mark territory
On deliberate position to copulate
Where the rod has a playmate
To exhibit and take aim a try
Oh! how far this pointer can fling

World wide your whacker
Agitates in wind speed
But when the poker becomes equipment
A striving see saw riding a frame
Till member tip nucleus drip
Then lcak polluted rain
Which drain nematodes, fornication
A pivot at the point leaves
A host not to be extracted
Among operatives who cultivate

I take you there.
enjoy.
Can you feel it?

MADAME MONSIEUR
SELLS SKUNK OIL

She roils as she recoils
an odor so scent-di- torious, polecat-lift
a stink to think whether

a sachet, cachet mixed
to bottle to topple or exit potential
for Mesdames Solicit-O, Monsieur Tax-O –
Bingo, SmellBender, PerfumeryMaster

rosettes to pass like gas,
Perfume up Iowa, Miami, Texas, Blue Grass
for some to wear masks to
diffuse news control or lose?

Sniff up/mockup the rules
for an aroma for fame touted
across special places of a polecat

with amour whose smell
makes you suck up to inhale.
What is not so obnoxious for sale?

POETIC VIBES:
DIATRIBES IN SEVEN

1

"Antipasto?"
No! "Anapestic!"

"Hmmmmmm!
I'll ask preceptor."

If staking out
This anapest
Should I be
Ex'treme to
In'ter'vene?
Or appear opined
To un'der'line?

Otherwise
To view
  the word
    should I
      travel the route
    to un'der'stand
The making
Of an anapest?

Oui! Oui! Si'Si'Si'
Do Ra! A petite mel'o'dee
Heehee! Hee'hee'hee!

2

Atliteration?
No! "An alliteration."

Is it sticky so icky?
Or a licky lucky deliberation?

"That drives one
'Smelly, 'Selly!
Into the planet
    Of 'shaky quaky jellies?"

3

Where his elegy of lore
Hungered tight bemused
No other place to go
Bemoans Whinnie's tale of woe

Anchored bottom upon a stool
He looked an extenuated fool.

He was heard to say

His plight had caused
Such neglect and fright
For his new bride
Of optic delight.

She appeared consumed in tears, drowned,
Blanched at the sight.
Her once lyrical voice,
Now spoiled, turned into
An inebriated whine

She joined him in his dote
On brew, loiter and smoke,
Forever the task convoked.

4

How does one stare at blank verse?
With the eye entranced.

What Should I look for?
Verse that does not rhyme.

Why this anomaly?
Informally may I scrawl in both?

We'll see.

Met a 'cool' yellow-jacket
On the gallery crawling,
In play I tried to engage
The intent to go straight.

But it wouldn't buy
So I jumped in front and in back
As I raised my foot to crush

I heard father caution "Don't"
Paid no heed.
So now I wear this swell upon the sole.

5

Assonance is my persona.
I wear it like a haberdasher
Which makes me a mad! Mad
hatter!

6

Just call me an oxymoron

"Calm as a viper."

7

Onomatopoeia

O Deity of the dark
We hear you vociferate
CawCaw! CawCaw! CawCawup!

While avifauna wait like olive
branches
Until from across,
They hear no more,
This "Caw Caw Caw Caw
Caw Caw Caw up"
As they exit from the bough.

CHILDREN FIVE FINGER PLAY

They bend on tiptoe
Five digits spin.
At play upon
Phonograph record spun
On an unplugged victrola

Whirls in frenzy
Heads in a shake
Toes in a tap
Tongues in a rap

While Mama did a clap clap
To the beat as she rolled dough
To make teacakes and s'mores

From this hut
No waterpower
To actuate this tune
Only five-finger spins

Faster and faster
Soon tunes would flow
Past the tinny tinny

As childlike sopranos begin to sing
By The waters of the Minnetonka
Splashes of puddles, imagined
Rush over brooks

Cross narrow runs
As it meanders
Five digits gyrate
Around the seventy-eight

WHAT'S ON THE TABLE
FOR THE LIZARD

I see you there
Lil' lizard king
As you slither
back and forth
on a lie around pad
of Magnolia leaves
Fig leaf lilies berry vines

To glide and slide
Upside down
Round and round
Lapping your tongue
As you speed

Lie in wait
Lick up creepy-crawlies
On the crawl
Or lie in wait
Upon a wall
A crack a lizard's stall

A Kiss But Never Like This

Tis' you I've known before
Who promised to come back
From that terrestrial ball in the sky
To land as a stud to nuzzle

Now memories linger, so

There you stood a mount upon a hill
Amidst clover and hay in an Iowa Field
Rays of light across your poll crest

Withers length barrel girth
Forehead raised as a light wind
Blew through nostrils flared to hold
Onto a scent blown before

Soon a gallop a trot
Toward me a soft clop clop
Then a muzzle nuzzle upon my neckline
Sending a quiver of surprise

''Twas you whom I've known before

i WOULD RATHER BE A-di-POSE, BUT iN A STATE OF RE-PO-SE

FOR WiLLiAM "BiLL" BRYSON

If you should ask, I will squeal
That I would rather bulge,
A character sketched,
Fattened to reveal

Just another hone of wit
To pick.

I'm a gassy-tro-no-me who opts
To wear a tent to disguise
What size one can become
If the intent is to parody a blimp.

Though a sight
Who might appear un-well,
Don't worry. It's just an outrance spell—

My Lament to ne'er-do-wells
Who flinch and squint at my swell.

Relinquish your envy
As to what I can engage
To arrive in such
An adipose stage

When upon my palate morsels
Placed mouthful to salivate,
Masticate:

Soufflé, bisque, brioches,
Krispy Kremes and other extremes—

Even a bird of any feast
Steeped wild with erotic exotic spices
Either smoked or baked until it's done

Jes' pitch me that drum-on-a-stick
Allow me to chomp on as quick?
As you can say.
"A vulture on a spit."

if i Should Die
Will i Go To Paradise
Or Dwell in An Oven Of Flames?

Worn headdress condemns
Displays some code-of-arms
Where isolation doesn't matter
When joining a one man
Power plant for gain, fueled

By moral laws of old men's game.
Who tutor youth in carnage
To hold claim to their aggression.

A classroom overseer's explosion
Invests bleak siren songs
An uneasy summit pushes unrest.

A wrap across breasts, a test
Clamps to seal mouths, a force,
Of legs uncrossed, locks into a vise:

No entrance here in this space
Where faces of Virgins are laced in shame
As icons of wickedness reigns.

JES' A CHEW FROM THE OL' WON'T DO, SPITTIN' QUESTIONS, SEEKING ANSWERS—

For Fence Sitters

I nod;
You nod.
Ain't nigh our needs,
Jes' a bunch of railings to lean on

Post to the masses.

Not even a chop on a stick
Would solve our fix

Still kneadin' that same soured
dough.

Stroke a body till it crumbles
Into 'sumptions of euphoria

When it's over
and crowds shift outside,
Obscurity rolls in and we be
still payin' our dues.

I say it's ah! brewin'
You say, "sho' is somethin'
But don't know what
Guess I'll jes' wait,"

PstShoo! Pstshoo! Nope!

Don't mind if I do
Mum! Ummm Yep! Hedging!

Don't mind if I do

Flowing

From pen to ink
I script words upon a page
Most often to take flight

Into language
Neither black nor white
Nevertheless a necessary fix

When efforts to nix
Rules over-rule
 A he/she/lit

In a world that superimposes, still
Between genders, shade, set
At will

O PEERLESS Child

Like a willow your limbs droop
With the weight of sorrow
Pressed against a back that
Packs a load of resistance

To well-being in all places
Where strife is the mask
Worn by those who mislead
Disfigure to kill children

In paddocks of poverty suffering
Neglect abuse branches cutoff
As you cry out a silence
In a forestation planted in pain

O how The Little Brown Man
Would Strut to the Beat Of The Bands
At The Des Moines Grand Avenue Parades

I never knew his name
Neither did many men
Women children, old skulls
Young and in-between heads

Yet our feet did a tap tap
As all hands did a clap clap
To the beat of the band
And the sight of the lil'brown man

As the bands played
When *The Saint's go Marching In*
The Star Spangle Banner
All those marching songs
Some old and some new

And you knew the lil'
Brown man who marched in sync
As if he were the leader
Of the parade
His baton he twirled
As his feet would step
From side to side in stride

All hearts would glow
Because they knew
That he marched from the core
Although no one had ask
Him to do so.

Just as duty had called for him to fight
In an era where separation was his plight

Although no stature in height
He was a patriotic sight
And the parade would have been amiss
Had he not been a participant in their midst

A PENNY MORE TO MAKE THEIR DAY

Boys on roller blades
Spin on a copper penny
Never to brake or decelerate
Accelerate without a glance

While on the sidewalks in
Downtown urban sprawl
Men in their suits to fit
Like bankers CEO-wanna-be's
Hopscotch around that one-center's shine
No stoop for a chance change

A maintenance mother walks
Holds onto her child's hand

Cautions
Don't pick it up

As the kid ask, why?

In her mind not worth the metal
It's stamped on
So they skip over

Second-rate Hank comes along
Wearing a hard hat of knocks
His eyes in a drop
Shoulders in a stoop as
He strolls daily loop-loop-de-loop
Round and round almost upside down
The crowded streets collecting
Any odds and ends found:
Beer cans pop bottles butts
Not always enough

But this day becomes a light bulb
When he finds a shiny copper coin
To add to chump change
Of four dollars and ninety-nine cents.

COMMON AS CORN THIS PORTRAYAL

When you sit around bars
Drink wine whiskey sours ales
Where fiction turns to protection groups

With your proline to proclaim
Identity with those who wear
A patch over the eye, a cap
Walk with a cane
Lost on an illusional train
Wearing a frame that is not pale

As long as they do not cross
Or move into your silo
The grain can be stored
In a faraway place anyplace

LONG IN TERM AND A WAIT FOR THE END
STILL CHALKING THE PAVEMENT

So many voices echo
On slave ships wherever the vessel
Docked to lure women children
With trinkets trophies chap rules
Allure for chaos of huge numbers
Toward disparagement

Disparity of a validation to cause rue in
Historical drama stages fear
For all who hear reverberations
Chap rules for chaos rules

A franchise long implementation:
A force to endure a thumping bumping
Superwomen making the news on
Covers that week-by-week dramatize
Their plight that leave them to moan

And I am still stationed on a slave ship
Looking for a mate inside a prison gate

TERROR BLAZES THE AIR

Everywhere before and now
Where winds blow chaos through
Cave mountain hovel street school

To throw the spear
Fire of gun
Death from hydrogen

Afterwards a pleasure practice
To snare those in the wake:
Women children innocents their take

As the discharge of masters
Runs through veins of those
At stake a spit of penile humour
Through victims own garments

Of virginity as a risk to lie
And wait for looters of glory

A WASH A WHIFF TO MAKE A BIG DAWG RUNAWAY YIPES! WOOF WOOF! GRRRRR! "WHITE SHOULDERS!...HEAD & SHOULDERS!"

Under dat' cone tree glowin' in da' dark,
strung wid' blinkers, ornaments & beads
I wuz sniffin' for aah' raw deal
ta' paw ta' chow down fer'a meal

Purina, bowzie nuts, purhaps a mutt biscuit
to make ma'retriever fur lush
but not a sniff of stink dat' makes
my snuffle turn downright, smell plight
dread, instead

again, she wanna' make me her big smelly dog
dat' jes'vexes and hexes me dis' time of year

"Hey Santa didn't' yo' get ma' riff?"
I've grown weary of dis'every Xmas gif'.

Her ruse as she brush and spray

"O Philippe darling, "she coos!" I'm goona'
have you smelling like a shoulder
to leave a scent on, oozes of sniff sniff!
So that Coco can get your drift."

This time around she don' gone too far
as soon as dat' dawg gone door is opened,
I'm outta here to join my mutt pals
who jes' luv' my muss.

SLURP! A DECLARATION OF WAR

Shllurrrpp! Trill thrill of a slurp
Japanese style, once a polite way
to eat hot noodles and other pasta fare

in a slurp-slurp manner, declares
an issue of war when one makes
noises while eating this tasteful mass.

Though a bit explosive, yet a polite
old way to dine or chow down
on this paste, a taste so delectable

short-circuits the stares
or those who seek to ignore
this noisy sloop-sloop of diner's food.

Those notes trill a sound
to enjoy a taste that makes you
sloop and slurp, ignoring a frown.

On the other hand, some whose attire
is of silk, Gucci's do styles,
and all other ilk might be inclined:

"Oomph! Excuse me, please,
a care that you do not sneeze-
I do not want spitter sputter spatter splatter

On my Gucci silk tie. It doesn't matter?
My Kimoni Sleeve?"

LITTLE BOY
WITH SKIN A CHARCOAL HUE

that illuminates through
day or night
as you play
run through streets
where pot holes
are a trench
so deep to slow
your speed
when all you want
is to lead
be hip with
style
to achieve
A flight to Mars
A walk on the moon
whistle a success
in a pocket tune

come with me
don't climb that dogbane tree
to make arrows
tipped with poison
that causes bleeds
that will create
a flow of doom

brothers die
mama's papa's cry
sisters alone await wail
their sorrow planted
on an abandoned trail

INDIGO BOY
EYES SO BROWN

Why do you wear
Such a worn-out frown
On that medicine head

Those cornrow locks
Braids that flop

A listening ear
Open with fear

Neither mama nor papa near
To spoon feed or fill a need

The whistle mute
The horn a hazy lazy toot

Boogity boogity to the store

Games by means of fatality
Bullets fly from door to door

A prison floor your score
A quiver shiver of woe

AMALGAMATION

Come taste the sugarcane
Harvest among the multitudes
Whose tongues are of many
To blend amalgamation
Rootstock to mitigate sourness
Planted in furrows of sweetness
Where steward of grains
Lift their foot to plow

Come taste the sugarcane
Pull your chair to the field
Fuse these past feuds
Unite sense with sorrow

Come taste the sugarcane — the last supper bell rings
Steady the shakers on a service set for tomorrow